D0953420

Hurts Like a Mother

Hurts Like a Mother

A Cautionary Alphabet

Jennifer Weiss and Lauren Franklin
Illustrated by Ken Lamug

Doubleday

New York • London • Toronto • Sydney • Auckland

Book design by Michael Collica
Jacket design by Michael J. Windsor
Jacket illustration by Ken Lamug

Library of Congress Cataloging-in-Publication Data
Weiss, Jennifer, 1968–
Hurts like a mother : a cautionary alphabet / by Jennifer Weiss and Lauren Franklin ;
illustrated by Ken Lamug.
pages cm
ISBN 978-0-385-54077-3 (hardcover) — ISBN 978-0-385-54078-0 (eBook)
1. Alphabet—Humor. 2. Alphabet books—Humor. I. Franklin, Lauren, 1969–
II. Lamug, Ken, 1978– illustrator. III. Title.
PN6231.A45W45 2016
818'.602—dc23
2015019204

MANUFACTURED IN CHINA

1 3 5 7 9 10 8 6 4 2

First Edition

For Charles—my loving husband and best friend—who has been forced to hear more rhymes about mothers than should be required of any person, and for my fabulous daughters, who provided absolutely no data for this book. I adore you all completely and wouldn't have it any other way.

—L.F.

For Leonard—my soul- and writing-mate—who, when reading this book, laughed in all the right places, and for Anya and Felix, who thankfully served as only minor inspiration for the contents herein. Without all of your abiding love and support, I might have been a casualty, too.

—J.W.

And for our own mothers—Andy and Olga—for whom we have even greater appreciation than before.

Hurts Like a Mother

Amy overdid the Pinot
at the Parent Potluck

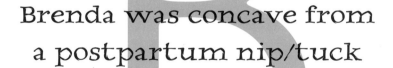

Brenda was concave from
a postpartum nip/tuck

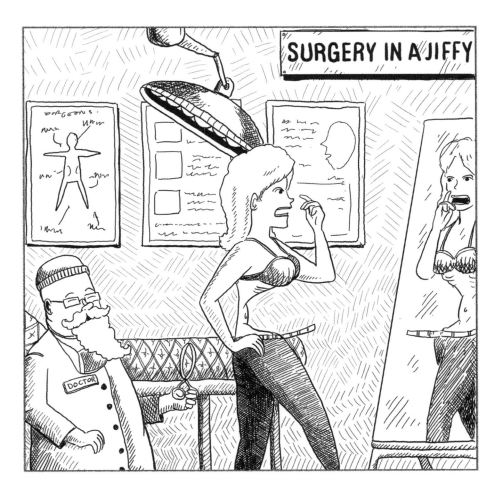

Claire was iced out--
her snacks weren't organic

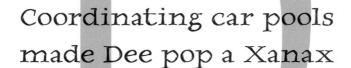

Coordinating car pools
made Dee pop a Xanax

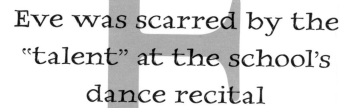

Eve was scarred by the "talent" at the school's dance recital

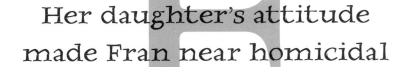

Her daughter's attitude
made Fran near homicidal

Gloria went blind searching for nits and head lice

Helen blacked out, eyeing
the American Girl's price

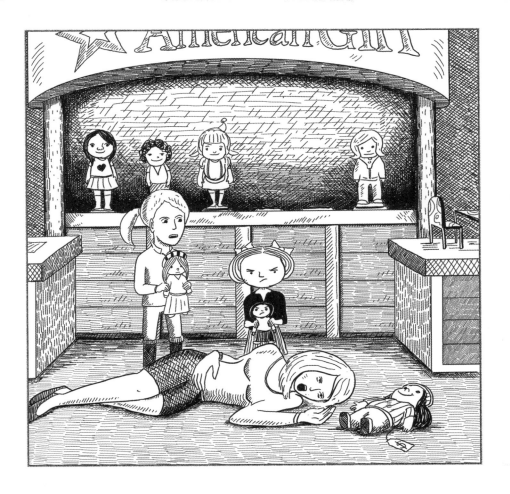

I

Ingrid was electrocuted
when her breast pump shorted

J

With the "family bed" arrangement, Jane's sex life was aborted

K

Kelly slit her wrists
chopping apples for a snack

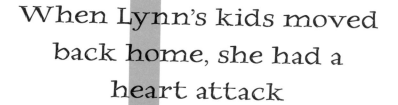

L

When Lynn's kids moved
back home, she had a
heart attack

M

An abundance of snow
days deflated Mary's esprit

N

Browsing parenting books,
Neve died of ennui

Olive got carpal tunnel
typing preschool applications

P

Paula broke down during
sex ed conversations

Queenie was flattened
running into heavy traffic

Ruby died of shame--
her son's texts: pornographic!

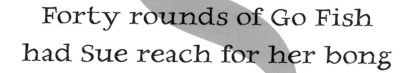

Forty rounds of Go Fish
had Sue reach for her bong

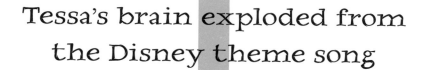

Tessa's brain exploded from
the Disney theme song

Una boiled with road rage
on the endless college tour

The formidable Tiger Moms
made Vera insecure

W

Inflating the pool toys led
to Wynne's asphyxiation

X

Xena's "mom jeans" caused her public humiliation

Y

Yvette burned to a crisp
toasting s'mores on the fire

Zoe couldn't take it--
she chose to retire

About the Authors

JENNIFER WEISS consults for nonprofits on public health policy, advocacy, and education and is the coauthor of *Brooklyn by Name: How the Neighborhoods, Streets, Parks, Bridges, and More Got Their Names* and *Citizen-in-Chief: The Second Lives of the American Presidents*. She lives in Brooklyn with her husband and two children.

LAUREN FRANKLIN lives in Washington, D.C., with her husband and two children.

Weiss and Franklin have been sharing dark humor for more than twenty-five years. Beyond their writing collaboration, they cofounded babyPolitico, a children's clothing company.